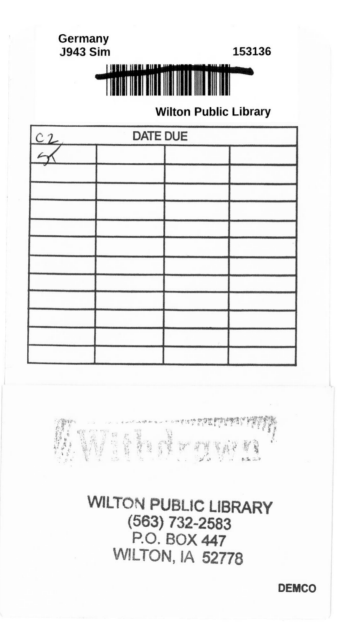

EXPLORING COUNTRIES

Germany

by Walter Simmons

BLASTOFF! READERS
5

BELLWETHER MEDIA • MINNEAPOLIS, MN

Note to Librarians, Teachers, and Parents:

Blastoff! Readers are carefully developed by literacy experts and combine standards-based content with developmentally appropriate text.

Level 1 provides the most support through repetition of high-frequency words, light text, predictable sentence patterns, and strong visual support.

Level 2 offers early readers a bit more challenge through varied simple sentences, increased text load, and less repetition of high-frequency words.

Level 3 advances early-fluent readers toward fluency through increased text and concept load, less reliance on visuals, longer sentences, and more literary language.

Level 4 builds reading stamina by providing more text per page, increased use of punctuation, greater variation in sentence patterns, and increasingly challenging vocabulary.

Level 5 encourages children to move from "learning to read" to "reading to learn" by providing even more text, varied writing styles, and less familiar topics.

Whichever book is right for your reader, Blastoff! Readers are the perfect books to build confidence and encourage a love of reading that will last a lifetime!

This edition first published in 2011 by Bellwether Media, Inc.

No part of this publication may be reproduced in whole or in part without written permission of the publisher. For information regarding permission, write to Bellwether Media, Inc., Attention: Permissions Department, 5357 Penn Avenue South, Minneapolis, MN 55419.

Library of Congress Cataloging-in-Publication Data

Simmons, Walter (Walter G.)
  Germany / Walter Simmons.
     p. cm. — (Exploring countries) (Blastoff! readers)
  Summary: "Developed by literacy experts for students in grades three through seven, this book introduces young readers to the geography and culture of Germany"—Provided by publisher.
  Includes bibliographical references and index.
  ISBN 978-1-60014-481-3 (hardcover : alk. paper)
  1. Germany—Juvenile literature. I. Title.
  DD17.S48 2010
  943—dc22   2010013643

Printed in the United States of America, North Mankato, MN.

080110   1162

Contents

Denmark

North Sea

Baltic Sea

Berlin ⭐

Netherlands

Germany

Belgium

Czech
Republic

↗
Luxembourg

France

Austria

Switzerland

Germany is a country in central Europe that covers 137,847 square miles (357,022 square kilometers). At one time, Germany was divided into West Germany and East Germany. The country is reunited today, and its capital is Berlin.

Germany has many neighbors. The Netherlands, Belgium, France, and the tiny nation of Luxembourg lie to the west of Germany. Switzerland and Austria are its southern neighbors. Germany touches Poland and the Czech Republic to the east. To the north, Germany borders Denmark, the Baltic Sea, and the North Sea.

Poland

Germany has many different land features. Northern Germany is flat. It has **wetlands**, plains, and rainy seacoasts. From the seashore, people can see small islands in the North and Baltic Seas. Hills, forests, and mountains cover southern Germany. The Alps rise along the country's southern border. Zugspitze, a mountain near Austria, is the highest point in Germany.

Many rivers flow through Germany's landscape. The second-longest river in Europe, the Danube, flows from its **source** in Germany's Black Forest. The Elbe River, with its source in the Czech Republic, crosses northern Germany before it empties into the North Sea. The Oder River forms part of Germany's border with Poland and ends at the Baltic Sea.

fun fact

Zugspitze stands about 9,721 feet (2,963 meters) tall. Hiking from the base of the mountain to the summit often takes several days.

Zugspitze

Did you know?

Many castles dot the German landscape. Neuschwanstein, a castle in southern Germany, was the inspiration for Disney's Sleeping Beauty castle.

The Rhine River

8

Germany's longest river is the Rhine. The source of this waterway is a lake in the Swiss Alps called Tomasee. From there, it flows north through Germany and then crosses into the Netherlands. Many castles are perched along the Rhine's steep riverbanks. Centuries ago, these castles protected the river valley from invaders. The castle lords also collected tolls from passing boats.

A **canal** links the Rhine to the Danube, which flows east through southern Germany. **Barges** and boats can travel all the way from the Black Sea in eastern Europe to the mouth of the Rhine.

fun fact

Lorelei Rock rises at the narrowest part of the Rhine in Germany. According to a legend, an angry woman lived on top of the rock. She sang to passing ships. Distracted by the beauty of her song, sailors crashed their ships into the rocks below.

grebe

Many different animals live in the forests and mountains of Germany. Foxes, red squirrels, rabbits, and small deer make homes in the woods. Wildcats chase wild boars across the forest floor. Chamois and ibexes live in the Alps along with wild sheep called mouflon.

wild boar

mouflon

northern
pike

! fun fact

The largest northern pike ever caught came out of an abandoned quarry in Dannstadt, Germany. The fish weighed 55 pounds (25 kilograms)!

Germany's seas and freshwater rivers and lakes are home to many creatures. Along the coasts, bird-watchers can spot loons, cranes, and diving grebes. The rivers and lakes hold trout, perch, pike, and other fish. Seals, dolphins, and sharks swim in the waters of the North and Baltic Seas.

fun fact

Lederhosen, or leather shorts with suspender straps, are part of traditional dress for German men and boys.

Over 82 million people live in Germany. German **ancestors** belonged to different **native** groups of eastern Europe. They moved west to Germany in search of better hunting grounds and farmland. Recently, **immigrants** have come to Germany from Italy, Poland, Greece, and other European countries.

Other people come from countries in North Africa and the Middle East. The largest non-native group in Germany comes from Turkey. Many immigrants speak their native languages, but most also speak German, which is Germany's official language.

Speak German!

English	German	How to say it
hello	hallo	HA-low
good-bye	auf wiedersehen	owf VEE-der-zay-en
yes	ja	yah
no	nein	nine
please	bitte	BIT-tuh
thank you	danke	DAHN-kah
friend	Freund	froind

In German cities, people head to work or school in the morning. They use cars, trains, and bikes to get around, and often shop in small markets for food. Many people also shop at **hypermarkets**, where they can buy groceries, clothing, games, furniture, and electronics. In the countryside, people live in homes near small villages or farms. Farmers rise early to tend to their crops or livestock. In both the cities and the countryside, families usually gather together for the evening meal, or *Abendessen*.

Where People Live in Germany

countryside
26%

cities
74%

fun fact

First graders in Germany receive huge cardboard cones, or *Schultütes*, on their first day of school. Family members decorate these cones and fill them with candy, toys, and school supplies.

In Germany, all children go to school between the ages of 6 and 15. Elementary school, or *Grundschule*, lasts four or six years. The number of years depends on where the student lives.

After elementary school, students can attend one of three different schools. A *Hauptschule* is a school for general studies. It prepares students for work. The other two kinds of schools prepare students for university. A *Realschule* teaches languages, science, math, and other subjects. A *Gymnasium* teaches similar subjects, but is much more rigorous.

Where People Work in Germany

manufacturing 29.7%

farming 2.4%

services 67.9%

Did you know?
Germany uses more wind power than any other country in the world except for the United States.

Germany has one of the strongest economies in Europe. In cities, factory workers make iron, steel, machinery, cement, chemicals, and cars. Many Germans have **service jobs** in banks, hospitals, or shops. Some drive taxis or operate trains that help people travel around Germany. Workers in restaurants and hotels offer their services to millions of travelers from around the world.

Farming, mining, and logging are important industries outside the cities. German farmers grow wheat, potatoes, fruits, cabbages, and other vegetables. Livestock farmers raise cattle, pigs, and **poultry**. Miners dig up coal and iron ore. Almost one-third of Germany is covered in forests. Loggers cut down trees and send them to mills where they are made into lumber, furniture, and paper products.

Playing

fun fact

One of the most famous athletes in Germany is Michael Schumacher. He is considered by many to be the world's most successful Formula One race car driver.

Germans spend their free time doing a variety of activities. Many people belong to sports clubs. These clubs play basketball, soccer, volleyball, and other team sports. There are also professional leagues for many of these sports in Germany.

Germans love the outdoors. They enjoy hiking and camping in Germany's many forests and mountain ranges. There are walking and biking paths all over the country. In winter, Alpine slopes challenge brave skiers and snowboarders.

fun fact

The bread pretzel, or *Brezel*, is a popular food in Germany. It is served with many meals and at festivals throughout the country.

German food is heavy and flavorful. Pork, **veal**, lamb, and beef are popular meats. Germans enjoy these meats as roasts and in meat **dumplings** and meat pies. They are often served with potatoes and vegetables such as cabbage, carrots, or asparagus. Germany is famous for its sausages. There are more than 1,000 different kinds of sausages in Germany. Germans also enjoy their desserts. Cakes and **tarts** are often made with apples, cherries, strawberries, and other fruits. These fruits are also used in puddings.

sausage

tart

Germans celebrate many public holidays. One of these is Unity Day, which takes place on October 3. On this day, Germans celebrate the reunification of their country in 1990. For Christian Germans, Christmas is an important religious holiday. In Germany, it is bad luck for children to see the Christmas tree until Christmas Eve. When the tree is finally decorated, a bell sounds. The children rush to see it and discover presents and candy underneath.

Unity Day

Christmas market

Following Germany's defeat in World War II, the country was divided into East and West Germany. Its capital was divided into East and West Berlin. American, French, and British troops occupied West Berlin. Troops from the **Soviet Union** controlled East Berlin. The government of East Germany had a wall built along its border with West Berlin. Nobody living in East Germany could enter West Berlin.

Did you know?

In the early 1980s, people on the west side of the Berlin Wall began covering it with graffiti. The wall's east side remained blank until the wall was torn down. People caught painting the east side could go to jail.

In 1989, Germans tore down the wall. They celebrated by dancing on top of the rubble. Germany reunited the following year. A few pieces of the wall remain to remind Germans of their nation's divided past and to give them hope for the future of their unified country.

Fast Facts About Germany

Germany's Flag

The flag of Germany shows three horizontal stripes. The top stripe is black, the middle stripe is red, and the bottom stripe is yellow. The colors represent modern, unified Germany and the freedom of its people. Germany first adopted the flag in 1919. It was readopted in 1949 after World War II.

Official Name: Federal Republic of Germany

Area: 137,847 square miles (357,022 square kilometers); Germany is the 62nd largest country in the world.

Capital City:	Berlin
Important Cities:	Munich, Hamburg, Cologne, Frankfurt, Stuttgart
Population:	82,282,988 (July 2010)
Official Language:	German
National Holiday:	Unity Day (October 3)
Religions:	Christian (68%), Other (32%)
Major Industries:	farming, forestry, manufacturing, mining, services
Natural Resources:	coal, copper, iron ore, natural gas, nickel, salt, uranium, wood
Manufactured Products:	cars, chemicals, electronics, metals, machinery, furniture, clothing, toys
Farm Products:	barley, sugar beets, hops, oats, potatoes, wheat, fruits, cabbages, cattle, pigs, poultry
Unit of Money:	euro; the euro is divided into 100 cents.

Glossary

ancestors—relatives who lived long ago

barges—large, flat boats used to carry heavy goods such as coal or grain up and down rivers

canal—a small trench dug across land that connects two bodies of water; canals allow ships to move between the two bodies of water.

dumplings—balls of dough filled with meat or vegetables

hypermarkets—giant stores where shoppers can find food, clothing, and household goods

immigrants—people who leave one country to live in another country

native—originally from a place

poultry—birds raised for their eggs or meat

service jobs—jobs that perform tasks for people or businesses

source—the place where a river begins to flow

Soviet Union—a former country in eastern Europe and western Asia; the Soviet Union broke up in 1991.

tarts—small pies made with fruit, custard, or jelly

veal—the meat of young cattle

wetlands—wet, spongy land; bogs, marshes, and swamps are wetlands.

To Learn More

AT THE LIBRARY

Blashfield, Jean F. *Germany*. New York, N.Y.:
Children's Press, 2003.

Byers, Ann. *Germany: A Primary Source Cultural
Guide*. New York, N.Y.: PowerPlus Books, 2005.

Russell, Henry. *Germany*. Washington, D.C.:
National Geographic, 2007.

ON THE WEB

Learning more about Germany
is as easy as 1, 2, 3.

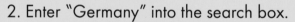

1. Go to www.factsurfer.com.

2. Enter "Germany" into the search box.

3. Click the "Surf" button and you will see a list of
   related Web sites.

With factsurfer.com, finding more information is just
a click away.

Index